BUTTERFLIES IN HEART

A POETIC TALE

PRITHA BHATTACHARYA

Dedicated to my Parents.

Also to my Grandparents, Friends, God and every element that is life.

Contents

Preface

As a young twelve-year-old in a small apartment in Jamshedpur, I was loitering around, trying to create a fancy card as a gift for my maternal grandparents' wedding anniversary. Sitting in the cool balcony breeze of the flat in the otherwise scorching summer heat and staring at the trees waving to the wind's music, I had a mini eureka moment of mine. I had words pouring and overflowing from my heart and a strong urge to pen them down. In no time, I had written my first poem, in Hindi, dedicated to the love of my grandparents, or at least how I interpreted it as a child. This seemingly ignorable incident started a series of many more such epiphanies and reflections wherein I would feel compelled to write.

I found my magic in twisting sentences and stitching ideas to express things beyond what mere words could convey. I believe I have captured how poetry makes me feel most beautifully in the following lines, which also happen to mark the start of one of my poems, later mentioned in this book:

> *"The bars of restriction do not exist in my reflections*
> *And so, when I think, in that moment*
> *I'm all free, liberated, unconfined and all content."*

With all that said, to all of you reading my dear book, I have a disclaimer. As much as I love poetry, I must accept -- I am a seasonal poet at best, someone who writes only when words intentionally come to me. Are you familiar with the butterflies in your stomach that wake up when you're way too excited or way too nervous? It is only when my heart is bustling with those same butterfly-ish jitters that I get blessed with the art of poetry. It is, therefore, more of a responsibility than a mere desire to capture these blessings in a more permanent form, which is what I have tried to do in this book. And if you haven't already figured it out, this is also exactly the reason why this book is named "Butterflies in Heart".

If I have not made it very obvious yet, this is my very first attempt at writing a book. This book is a small collection of my poems that I like the most. Many of them were written when I was too young to appreciate my craftsmanship. Looking back at them, I see the potential they held and the deeper meanings embedded in their subtle pauses and abrupt line breaks. Some poems are relatively newer, written with full consciousness and awareness of the craft and what it symbolizes.

I hope you have a good read and I hope you find the meaning in the lines as well as between the lines of my poetry.

1. Love & Memories

A lyrical composition displaying a lover figuring out that her love is very different from the conventional expectations that she had built over the years. Our lover gives in to this new found definition and finds her peace in the imperfections and clauses of love that she has discovered. She still retains and expresses her passion for holding on to her feelings.

Love might fade but memories wouldn't
We might lie but our hearts shouldn't.
I'd always known love as something permanent
Something to hold on to and spend a lifetime with
Something that gives you a reason, a purpose
Something that gives you the strength, the guts and the nerves
To face life and deal with its atrocities
And to live life and enjoy its ludicrousities.
I've now come to see this love in a new light
And I understand when you say that it might fade
And I agree when you say we might grow apart
And I relate when you say it'll be an inevitable psychological
change that'll play with our hearts
And while we seem to be on the same page
I still believe that I should love you as hard as I can

And hold on to you for as long as I can
And make you my reason, make you my purpose
Be your strength and be the reason you smile
The reason you're brave and the reason you're mine.
I am willing to go through a heartbreak
Take a deep breath
But I cannot not love you anymore baby.
I can only wish that we spend a lifetime watching the moon
and catching the stars and jumping the space with my fingers
entwined in the gap of yours
Gently swirling my thumb on the top of your palms
Feeling your pulse, a heartbeat at a time
As we close our eyes for the last time
As we know each other for one last time
As we smell each other in one last breath
And as we become the stars we once chased.

2. You

A short poem capturing the butterflies in the heart of our lover who has fallen head over heels and can just not stop thinking about her muse.

I could stare at the sea waves
Or look into infinity
Gasp at the depth of the sky
Or marvel at the bird's serenity
No matter what I do
No matter where I see
Be it the wind gushing by
Or the smile of a child's glee
It is you I think of
You I adore
Your memories I recall
And you I live for.

3. I hope

A lyrical self-talk composition displaying an intense chaos in the mind of our lover, who was too attached, who held on too tightly. That, until she could no more. This poem captures the moment she snaps and talks herself through it, realising that probably all that is happening is indeed for the best. This is not a moment of breaking up, but rather a moment of letting go.

It is not love that backs out.
And so, I let him go.
Liberated him of all the strings that join us.
Rendered him free, carefree. Burdenless.
He could no more be fed up of me.
I could no more disappoint him.
There is no more a vice in me that could make him unhappy.
He could no more resent me.
Because isn't this all that I would ever want from him?
One eye full of respect for me,
And the other full of happiness and satisfaction in life?
Isn't this what I was always striving for while I held all the strings tightly and very cautiously so that I don't end up breaking them?

Well, I did not break them.

They got entangled.

Just like our miserable lives that got entangled with and kept choking each other.

I couldn't keep the strings safe. I failed.

But holding on to messed-up strings could've resulted in one of them breaking.

And I couldn't let any string break.

So I let them loose.

I set them free.

I set him free.

Of all his responsibilities and of all his accountabilities.

Of all his love and his forced emotions.

I set him free.

He was a force to be reckoned with.

A man who changed everything.

Everything about the very way I saw myself and my life.

Everything about how I dealt with things.

And everything about me.

But the one thing he couldn't change in me,

Was this constant desire to see him happy.

To not let the strings break.

To not let the world lose its hopes in humanity.

To be there for all the silent sufferers and to be against all the loud victors.

He changed everything about me and around me, but he couldn't change me.

I survived the force he came with.

I survived the fire and the storm he came with.

I feel so wholesome now.

I feel so grown up now.

I'm proud I didn't let the strings break.

Since I have set them free now, I hope they will untangle themselves.

I hope he will be happy always.

I hope I will find my peace above him.

Because I know for sure that,

It is not love that backs out.

And I didn't.

And I survived.

And I set him free.

And so I hope,

Everything will be for the best.

I hope, I hope.

I hope for the best.

4. Time Swings

A short composition displaying how, with changing time and changing perceptions, an explorer's view of herself also changes, often rendering her clueless about who she really is. This poem captures the beginning of a new realisation and development of the desire to escape from it.

That, and much more, open to multiple interpretations.

Done and undone in a moment,
Kept and left to be in another,
The time keeps flying away
With no more a moment to bother.
Vicious cycles of passionate love and extreme hate
Trying to ensure gaiety,
I feel I am lost in the world and in my naivety.
Assist me in breaking the bars, help me set myself free
Emancipation is all I demand; let the whole world reflect my glee.

5. Arrested in Time

The theme of discovering an identity crisis is further developed in this poem wherein our explorer feels puzzled and powerless with all the thinking and over-thinking she has been doing and shows her desperation at not being able to fit in the world's expectations.

I look left, I look right
In the front, and even behind
Cold red eyes is all I see
Everywhere around me and in my mind.
Eyes that have caught my imagination,
eyes that have frozen my dreams
There is no purpose in breaking free
and I don't know how to leave.
I am arrested in time, at crossroads with myself.
I keep figuring out what I am not, but what am I even
supposed to be?
Nothing feels like me.
I am the oval head trying to fit in the square peg
Looking forward to the stage of life and waiting to break a leg.
I hold my breath in anticipation,
fear making rookie mistakes;
I am no more a force to reckon with,

I feel powerless in my headspace.

I no more know myself

or what I want, or what I need

Confrontations scare me, time doesn't pay any heed.

The clock keeps striking and minutes pass away

With each passing second, hopes and dreams ebb away.

I can't work, I can't rest

I am trying to write but my lines don't even rhyme

I am absolutely clueless and I feel arrested in time.

6. At the dusk's mercy

Our explorer has found her friend amidst all the chaos. And her de-light is not in 'the light' but instead in the darkness. This poem elaborates on why she resonates more with darkness than with light.

You pretend to be the Messiah of ultimate light
You preach bright words to illuminate the darkest of the souls
You say your rays will end the eternal darkness
And you equate gleam with the happiness
And there you are, proclaiming that luminiscence is indeed the way out
And there you are, allying radiance with hope and positivity with your assuring shout
And then there is this world that buys all that you expound
That believes you and equates darkness to evil and the depressed and the hounds
Now from where I stand and see, darkness is indeed the ultimate glee
It pacifies the heart that burns in your brilliance
It soothes the ones who are exhausted of the fake pretence
It's a blanket to warm the cold hearts and a patient listener to all the wet eyes

Trust me, the night has heard the worst of our cries.

Darkness is a friend to our aching souls

It mends and heals and gives strength to face the bright sun again

Gloom is where happiness actually began.

It's true that the day is just a masquerade while darkness is peace

Darkness is home, darkness is where de-light usually is

So no matter what you would like to believe

The world will someday know that

The dawn is always at the mercy of the dusk in the world we live.

7. The beginning

The prisoner waits for his turn to break free. This poem explores his joy of liberation. Liberation from the handcuffs, misery and the games of mind.
Or you could see this as our explorers liberation from the overthinking streak she has lately been on, open to multiple interpretations.

Handcuffed in a jail of unfulfilled dreams, misery awaits.
Failure-smeared destinies await the break of dawn,
The dawn breaks the silence of the mourning,
It is a new day, they say; A new beginning.
Shrill cries of the past, biting numbness of the space,
The deafening silence of his mind where words cease to play.
Breezing, sailing through this misery comes a ray of mirth,
A ray that rips apart the gloom, a ray that satiates the brain.
All was thus not in vain, the vanquished handcuffs scream his glee,
This, my lord of joy, was his chance to break free.
The hopes have now returned, so have the prayers, wishes and dreams,
He is now a free soul sir, his courage did destroy his melancholy.

• 13 •

8. Dance of life

Our explorer elaborates on her tight-roping skills, balancing various aspects of life, and realizes she can keep herself occupied in everyday tasks without really wondering about her identity. This poem explores how she comes to terms with the fact that although this momentary liberation feels relieving, change being the only constant, she will eventually have to face her fears and find her identity to hold her ground in the dance of life.

I dance to the beats of life
With two left feet and nothing ever going right
I sway (a bit awkward)
Balancing the whites and the greys
The blacks aren't visible in my world's ways.
I am shielded in my rose universe
but improvement is all I strive
I am aware the protection is temporary
As change, is the only constant in life.

9. In Times of Pandemic

This poem was written in the COVID summer with a very dear friend and a poet himself, Aabhas Amol. There are days when you start a work and don't know how to finish it. Aabhas helped me finish this one, he gave the poem its much needed closure to make it the beautiful piece it today is.

This poem brings forth the subtle nuances of complicated situations like pandemics wherein despite all the sadness all around us, reflecting deeply within us we can often find an abundance of good deeds that help in keeping the hopes high. It elaborates on how the most inhumane conditions often help in bringing forth the best in humanity.

The bars of restriction do not exist in my reflections
And so, when I think, in that moment
I am all free, liberated, unconfined and all content.
The world is static now, nothing seems to budge
But I'm used to seeing it this way
As reflections never move.
Gazing at the globe with my rose coloured glasses,
I see people. One at a time;
Rediscovering compassion, friendship and peace in solitude
The feelings that seemed lost

Are suddenly all my vision sees, feels

Good deeds abound in silence's euphonies,

I wonder if I am simply hallucinating in the name of epiphanies.

The masquerading has come to an absolute halt

With people baring their selves in the comfort of their homes

She isn't afraid to be herself anymore

He knows in this fight he is never alone.

But, despite the harmony in this united front,

The souls in my reflection look all empty and lonely

They have come to realise that this might indeed be the end of the world

Or the end of the way we have known it.

Away from our loved ones, locked down in our homes.

A storm may be brewing, approaching menacingly,

But the human spirit proceeds unflinchingly

I feel the fire inside, burning bright. Joy not lost.

My reflections smile back at me

Dancing at the rhythm of small talk.

Giving hope anew,

Not God. Not the miracle men. But us.

You and I. Standing toe to toe together.

Matching step for step.

Bringing this world of ours

Piece by piece together.

With new stories to tell,

Memories to make, and

Life to be loved.

10. No Lavishness

A mini poem celebrating all the rich souls of the world living their lavish, non-materialistic, borderline heroic lives. Thank you for all your service to humanity!

She sat by the fire,
She danced along the street;
She toured the whole city on her bare feet
Doing meagre acts of kindness.
She lived a lavish life
Without a pinch of lavishness.

11. Attempts at Hindi Poetry

At the beginning of this book I had mentioned my first poem, a Hindi poem composed on the wedding anniversary eve of my grandparents. Although this book is a compilation of my top ten favorite English poems from the valuts, I thought of keeping a note of a few special Hindi ones as well, as a memoir if nothing else. I present here three of my favorite ones --

"Dil ka Sandesha" is the one celebrating love. This is the first poem I have ever drafted and the only one that I could recite while sleeping for a very long time. It is a special poem, marking the beginning of a beloved hobby for me.

"Ek Tara" is the second poem, composed immediately after the first one. Same day, just moments apart. It often doesn't get the credit it deserves. It is the more reflective poem, touching themes of despair, hopes and companionship. It is a reflection of how I perceived complex emotions as a child. It is a special poem as seconds deserve equal appreciation and celebrations as the firsts.

"Kar Parishram" is a fairly recent one. Heavily inspired by Harivansh Rai Bachhan sir's writing style and full of motivation and drama, it is a special poem as it marked a return to Hindi poetry in some ways for me.

Dil ka Sandesha

Dil se aaya ek sandesh kuch gehra
Jaise neel gagan me khile ek phool sunehra
Sandesha laaya thoda sneh aur thoda pyaar
Saath me aayi ek nayi bahar
Is sandesh ko tum gale se lagaana
Buri nazar apni is par tum mat chidkaana
Ise bhula kar pachtaaoge tum
Ise dhoond na paaoge tum
Dil ka yah sandesha tha mere pyaar ka
Meri betaabi mere intezaar ka
Jab ki thi maine is kavya ki rachna
Dil me mere tha bas ek hi sapna
Mujhe tum samajh humesha paao
Aur sada mere hi ho jaao

Ek Tara

Door kahin ambar me chipa ek taara
Sabse nyaara aur dil bhar pyaara
Dekh use mai sochu ab tab
Kahan se aaya yah neela taara aur kab
Doordeshi yah neela taara mujhe yaad dilaata meri baat

Mere akelepan ki kahaani din raat

Jab chaaha tha maine is neel gagan me mit jaane ko

Magar tabhi ek saathi ne haath mera pakda jo

Saathi saath me laaya pyaar saadhgi aur humdum

Chha gayi khushiyaan, mit gaye ab saare ghum

Sun re mere taare maine jaana hai tera kal

Chalte chalte yah kathor raaste aayega khushiyon ka bhi ek
anokha pal

Jee le thoda aur is pal ko ghut ghut ke

Itihaas ke panne par rach de ise apne andaaz me.

Kar Parishram

Maine kuch waqt pehle ek pran liya

Aur ki kadhi tapasya

Maine apni jwaala ko jalaaye rakha

Bujhne nahi diya iraado ka diya.

Ab bhi thodi aag bachi hai mujhme

Jal kar dhuaan ban jaana hai

Apni manzil ko paaye bina

Na sona hai na bujhna hai.

Yahi mehnat to ek din apna rang laayegi

Aur us din ka mujhe khub intezaar hai

Us din ke sapno se hi to aaj ka har ek kshann gulzaar hai.

Tapasya ka koi ant nahi

Ichhaon ki koi seema nahi
Par jo thaan liya so thaan liya
Kar ke dikhlaane ka josh yahi
Sar jhuka, dhyaan laga
Tera parishram hi antar laayega
Bas tu haar mat, tu bujh mat, tu jhuk mat
Har baadha ko haste haste yun hi paar kar jaayega.

www.ingramcontent.com/pod-product-compliance
Lightning Source LLC
Chambersburg PA
CBHW031254130726
47988CB00008B/3351